Quick Guide to ANIME and MANGA

Robert M. Henderson

ReferencePoint Press

San Diego, CA

About the Author

Robert M. Henderson has worked as an editor and copywriter for more than thirty years. He is the author of *National Geographic's World Regions: West Asia*; *The Spread of Hate and Extremism*; and *The Rise of Social Media: Shaming and Bullying*. He currently lives in Vermont.

Picture Credits:
Cover: 963 Creation

6: Maury Aaseng
10: The Stapleton Collection/Bridgeman Images
15: Photofest
21: REDXIII/Shutterstock.com
28: cOO7/Shutterstock.com

30: MBlackbunny/Shutterstock.com
34: Everett Collection
38: ADV Films/Photofest
41: Funimation Films/Photofest
44: nasrudin nur isnaini
50: portishead1/iStock
52: Mahathir Mohd Yasin

LIBRARY OF CONGRESS CATALOGING-IN-PUBLICATION DATA

Names: Henderson, Robert M., author.
Title: Quick guide to anime and manga / by Robert M. Henderson.
Description: San Diego, CA : ReferencePoint Press, 2021. | Includes bibliographical references and index.
Identifiers: LCCN 2020057733 (print) | LCCN 2020057734 (ebook) | ISBN 9781678200923 (library binding) | ISBN 9781678200930 (ebook)
Subjects: LCSH: Comic books, strips, etc.--Japan--Juvenile literature. | Animated films--Japan--Juvenile literature. | Animated television programs--Japan--Juvenile literature.
Classification: LCC PN6790.J3 H46 2021 (print) | LCC PN6790.J3 (ebook) | DDC 741.5/952--dc23
LC record available at https://lccn.loc.gov/2020057733
LC ebook record available at https://lccn.loc.gov/2020057734

CONTENTS

INTRODUCTION

Setting New Records

On October 16, 2020, Japanese filmgoers brushed aside concerns about the coronavirus pandemic to go see the animated film *Demon Slayer: Mugen Train*. More than 3.4 million people—close to 3 percent of the total population of Japan—saw the film over its opening weekend, the best opening in Japanese box office history. The film is expected to become the highest-grossing film in Japanese history, surpassing Hayao Miyazaki's 2001 film *Spirited Away*.

Before the film version, *Demon Slayer* was a massively popular manga, selling over 100 million copies worldwide. In 2019 it became an equally successful anime television series—also with an international following. All versions of *Demon Slayer* are famous for their stunning art, especially in the exhilarating and unique fight scenes. Many fans are also attracted to the darker tone the story can take on at times.

The story of *Demon Slayer* takes place in Japan during the early 1900s. It revolves around the adventures of Tanjiro Kamado, a young man who is on a quest to restore the humanity of his demonic sister Nezuko. The series attracts a diverse audience because of its charming characters, amazing action, and heartfelt, tear-jerking scenes. "I think a big part of its appeal is that it's very emotional," says Alfred Toh of the anime website Mipon. "It's very easy to understand, too."[1]

Not even the potential risk of attending a film during a deadly pandemic was enough to keep faithful fans away. Based on a survey, most moviegoers felt safe in the theater. "As soon as we got there, I felt quite reassured," said one fan. "We all had to have our temperature taken before we could go into the auditorium, we were told we had to wear a mask at all times and there was hand sanitizing liquid at every entrance."[2] Drinks were allowed in the theater, but no food.

The huge success of the *Demon Slayer* film far exceeded the expectations of film industry experts. Perhaps people just wanted to do something that seemed normal after nine months of disruption due to the pandemic. Makoto Watanabe, a professor of media and communications at Hokkaido Bunkyo University, says, "I think plenty of people will walk out of the cinema and identify with Tanjiro because our lives today often seem like one long struggle against monsters of one kind or another."[3]

> "Our lives today often seem like one long struggle against monsters of one kind or another."[3]
>
> —Makoto Watanabe, a professor of media and communications

A Uniquely Japanese Art Form

Demon Slayer is popular all over the world, but there was a time when manga and anime were completely unknown to people outside Japan. Japanese artists started producing modern-day manga during the mid-1900s. The word *manga* means "whimsical pictures" and refers to all Japanese comics. Like all Japanese books, manga books read from right to left, the reverse of English, and are usually printed in black and white. There are many genres of anime and manga, including science fiction, romance, horror, action and adventure, sports, comedy, and more.

How to Read Manga

In English, people read from left to right. In traditional Japanese manga, the action and dialogue move from right to left. This manga illustration shows the correct way to read the panels and word bubbles, beginning in the upper right-hand corner with 1A.

Anime is Japanese animation. Once a manga series gets popular, it is usually adapted into an anime. Anime is not just cartoons for kids. Much of it is aimed at older audiences. Takamasa Sakurai, a famous Japanese culture and anime expert, says, "Japanese anime broke the convention that anime is something that kids watch."[4]

Comics in the United States often feature superheroes who save the world, such as Iron Man or Wonder Woman. These types of heroes are not as popular in Japanese comics. Anime and manga usually feature realistic heroes and heroines, even if the rest of their lives are anything but ordinary. The artwork is also different from American comics. For example, Japanese artists often draw detailed close-ups of faces. They also exaggerate the emotional expressions of characters, who might suddenly change shape to show how they are feeling. To express anger, for example, a character might grow fangs while shouting at someone, but this does not necessarily alter the realism of the story.

"Japanese anime broke the convention that anime is something that kids watch."[4]

—Takamasa Sakurai, a Japanese culture and anime expert

A Global Phenomenon

Today, anime and manga are surging in popularity, both in Japan and in other countries. The global anime market size was valued at almost $21 billion in 2018 and is predicted to reach $36 billion by 2025, according to Grand View Research. This astonishing growth is largely due to the increasing availability of anime and manga outside Japan. Popular streaming video services such as Netflix, Amazon, and Hulu now carry many of the most popular anime titles. "Streaming overall has created a new wave of accessibility and discover-ability for anime,"[5] says John Derderian, Netflix's director of content for anime.

In the past, anime and manga were often seen as something that only hard-core fans could enjoy, but there is a broader acceptance in the United States today. This has allowed anime and manga to reach previously untapped audiences. "What's been really great to see, especially in the last two years, is this continued movement of mainstreaming of anime,"[6] says Joellen Ferrer, the head of communications at Crunchyroll, another service that streams anime.

Anime and manga are two of the most popular forms of entertainment in the world today. They bring in billions of dollars in revenue while appealing to people of all ages, genders, and nationalities. It is an incredible success story, but it did not happen overnight. Anime and manga have been at the heart of Japanese culture for decades and have much older roots than many fans realize.

CHAPTER 1

Origin Story

The history of anime and manga began a thousand years ago. During the eleventh century in Japan, a priest and artist named Toba Sojo made fun of his Buddhist colleagues by drawing them as cute, mischievous animals. His drawings featured frogs, rabbits, toads, and monkeys engaging in silly human activities (including farting contests). Toba Sojo painted on long rolls of paper called scrolls. Although there is no dialogue in his paintings, they do tell a story as the scroll is unfurled from right to left. These scrolls have been designated as a National Treasure of Japan and can be seen today in the Kozan Temple in Kyoto, Japan.

The term *manga* was first used in 1814 by the famous Japanese artist Katsushika Hokusai. His collection of sketches, called the *Hokusai Manga*, includes thousands of cartoon-like images of people, animals, plants, landscapes, and even demons and monsters. This book was not only a best seller in Japan, but it also became popular in Europe, where it influenced artists such as Édouard Manet, Claude Monet, and Edgar Degas. In 1831 Hokusai created what is arguably the world's most famous piece of Asian art: *The Great Wave*. The drawing shows a huge wave just as it is about to crash down on some fishing boats. Tim Clark, the head of the Japanese section at the British Museum, writes, "I've come to wonder if [Hokusai] wasn't one of the most

The Great Wave, *a drawing created in 1831 by Japanese artist Katsushika Hokusai, is arguably the world's most famous piece of Asian art.*

important inventors of modern animation. . . . Because of the way [*The Great Wave*] is so imaginatively composed, we feel an incredible surge of energy in the sea from right to left and on up into the wave."[7]

As the twentieth century dawned in Japan, Western culture began to increasingly influence Japanese art and manga. This influence became especially powerful after World War II, when thousands of US soldiers occupied Japan from 1945 to 1952. During this time, Japanese culture, including manga, was strongly shaped by American comics, television, film, and cartoons, particularly those of Disney.

The Godfather of Anime and Manga

What is now considered modern manga really began to emerge during the period right after World War II. And it was largely because of a single manga artist and animator: Osamu Tezuka. His innovations and pioneering techniques have earned him the nicknames "the God of Manga and Anime" and "the Japanese Walt Disney."

Born in 1928, Tezuka amazed all his schoolmates with his drawing abilities. After working in a factory as a teenager during the war, Tezuka moved to Tokyo to pursue a career drawing manga. He often found himself going to the movies for inspiration. When Disney's *Bambi* was released in Japan in 1951, Tezuka liked it so much that he saw it more than eighty times.

In 1951 Tezuka created one of manga and anime's most iconic and enduring characters—Astro Boy. The manga was so popular that Tezuka turned it into an animated television show, which became a huge hit in 1963. This was the first time a manga was adapted for television. It was also the first time a foreign cartoon became popular in America as well.

Astro Boy tells the story of a little robot boy who is built by a scientist when his own son dies in a car accident. When the scientist realizes that the robot can never replace his lost son, he sells Astro Boy to the circus. Fortunately, Astro Boy is saved by Professor Ochanomizu, who discovers that the boy robot has in-

The Lion King Controversy

Disney's *The Lion King* opened to rapturous audiences and critics in 1994. Although the film was supposed to be entirely original, many people claimed that it stole ideas from a manga called *Jungle Emperor*, which had been created in 1950 by the legendary Osamu Tezuka.

For example, the villain in *The Lion King* is an evil lion named Scar. In *Jungle Emperor*, the villain is an evil lion named Claw. Scar has a scar over his right eye, whereas Claw has a scar over his *left* eye. One of the most famous scenes in the movie is when Simba's father, Mufasa, materializes in the clouds. *Jungle Emperor* also has a scene where the lion father appears to his son in the clouds. The two scenes are "too similar to be a coincidence," says Frederik Schodt, the author of several books on Japanese manga.

Disney insists that no one involved with creating *The Lion King* was aware of *Jungle Emperor* or Tezuka. After some back and forth, the controversy ultimately fizzled out. "Because as much as Tezuka is considered important, the Japanese love Disney," says Yasue Kuwahara, a professor at Northern Kentucky University. "They recognized *Lion King* was a copy of *Jungle Emperor*, but it was OK with them."

Quoted in Pete Keeley, "Big Little Lions: Disney's New 'Lion King' Dodges the 'Kimba' Similarity Issue," *Hollywood Reporter*, July 22, 2019. www.hollywoodreporter.com.

credible superpowers and can experience human emotions. With the professor's help, Astro Boy helps save the world by fighting evil robots. Heavily influenced by Disney films, Tezuka drew Astro Boy with large, expressive eyes and cute features, just like a Disney character. Huge eyes and cute features are still found on the faces of many anime characters today.

One of Tezuka's most important innovations was to make manga more cinematic. He felt that the manga of his time was not interesting enough visually, so he worked hard to add lots of movement, action, and drama to his drawings. In his autobiography, he writes, "I felt [after the war] that existing comics were limiting. . . . Most were drawn . . . as if seated in an audience viewing a stage where actors emerge from the wings and interact. This made it impossible to create dramatic or psychological effects, so I began to use cinematic techniques. . . . French and German movies that I had seen as a schoolboy became my model."[8]

Tezuka's legacy is impossible to overstate. He almost single-handedly invented Japanese anime and helped it become popular internationally. Besides *Astro Boy*, some of Tezuka's most well-known works include *Phoenix*, *Dororo*, *Buddha*, *Princess Knight*, *Metropolis*, and *Kimba the White Lion*.

The Rise of the Blockbuster

Anime and manga continued to gain in popularity through the 1960s and into the 1970s. When the film *Star Wars* became an international sensation in 1977, Japanese artists started to focus more on science fiction and fantasy. Soon, one of the most popular television shows in Japan was *Gundam*, which premiered in 1979. Set far into the future, the story revolves around a war between the Earth Federation and the space colony Zeon. When Earth is attacked by Zeon robots, a young teenager named Amuro Ray must learn to operate the Earth Federation's new secret weapon: a giant humanoid robot called the Gundam. The success of the series led to many manga and anime sequels, prequels, side stories, and alternate timelines. It also spawned a whole industry of plastic models called Gunpla. Since it premiered, *Gundam* has generated $20 billion in total revenue, which makes it one of the highest-grossing media franchises of all time.

Five years later, another blockbuster anime series debuted: *Dragon Ball*. Based on a popular manga series, *Dragon Ball* follows the adventures of a boy named Son Goku, who spends most of his time training in the martial arts. A teenage girl named Bulma encourages him to search for the seven magical orbs called Dragon Balls. After all the Dragon Balls have been collected, a dragon appears that grants one wish. For many fans outside Japan, *Dragon Ball* was their introduction to anime. "*Dragon Ball* was the first of its kind," writes media journalist Craig Elvy. It was a "gateway into a world of animation vastly different to what western audiences were accustomed to . . . in an era where there was little else on TV to rival it."[9]

Simulcasting

Many anime fans like to watch simulcasts of their favorite new shows. This means they like to watch their shows on the exact same day as the original Japanese broadcast (a "simultaneous broadcast"). On streaming sites such as Crunchyroll, the lag behind Japanese broadcasts is usually by a few hours. Why that long? Because it takes time to translate and add subtitles to the episodes. Nevertheless, the process must be done very quickly. It involves a highly coordinated effort, with employees working at all hours of the day and night to finish episodes. Crunchyroll's ability to simulcast is a major reason why 2 million subscribers have signed up with the service.

Netflix has not embraced simulcasting as much, which angers many fans. They use the term *Netflix jail* to describe the wait between the original Japanese broadcast and eventual Netflix release. Sometimes it takes several months before a popular new anime is broadcast. As one frustrated fan tweeted, "Netflix jail for anime remains the single dumbest conscious design decision a streaming platform could make." Netflix argues that it must translate, dub, and subtitle an episode in over thirty different languages before it can be internationally released. Crunchyroll, meanwhile, only does nine languages.

Quoted in Jacob Robinson, "What Is 'Netflix Jail' and Why It Puts Netflix at a Disadvantage," What's on Netflix, August 12, 2020. www.whats-on-netflix.com.

Around this time, anime began to make an impact on the big screen as well as on television. In 1988 the film *Akira* was released. At the time, it was the most expensive anime film ever made, and it was like nothing the world had seen before. Visually stunning, violent, and relentlessly energetic, the film took animation to new heights. Set in a postapocalyptic "Neo-Tokyo," the convoluted plot involves a motorcycle gang of thrill-seeking teens who accidentally stumble upon a secret government-run project dealing with telekinetic powers in children. Film critic Stephen Hunter of the *Baltimore Sun* writes that *Akira* "is a blast and a half, a twisted dystopian parable of violence and rock and roll, Japanese-style. It's Disney on PCP, mean, rotten, psychotic, but incredibly vivid."[10] After its release, *Akira* created tremendous interest in manga, anime, and Japanese popular culture throughout the Western world. It also influenced countless films, comics, television shows, and video games.

Akira made many Western filmgoers and critics take notice of anime for the first time. But *Akira* was not the only Japanese film to get attention in 1988. A very different kind of anime—*My Neighbor Totoro*, directed by Hayao Miyazaki—also received rave reviews and became a worldwide sensation.

The Global Emergence of Studio Ghibli

Miyazaki is one of the most famous and beloved animators in the world. Born in 1941 into a family whose factory manufactured parts for Japanese fighter planes, his first memories are of fleeing his hometown due to American firebombing raids during the last days of World War II. Growing up in postwar Japan, he saw firsthand its rapid growth and industrialization. These experiences made a deep impression on Miyazaki, whose films often contain anti-war and proenvironmental themes.

As a boy, Miyazaki often read books with strong female characters. This influenced his films, which often feature girls or old women in leading roles. The main protagonist in Miyazaki's 1984 science fiction adventure film *Nausicaä of the Valley of Wind* is a charismatic, intelligent young princess who is a skillful fighter.

Set in a postapocalyptic future, the film tells the story of the last surviving humans who live in a barren landscape slowly being overtaken by what is known as the Toxic Jungle. Princess Nausicaä is able to communicate with the massive insects that live in this poisonous jungle, and with their help, she helps bring peace and prosperity back to the ravaged planet. The film was a huge success and led to the establishment of a new animation studio cofounded by Miyazaki: Studio Ghibli.

Miyazaki and Studio Ghibli's next film, *My Neighbor Totoro*, became an even bigger international hit. The film tells the story of two young sisters who encounter friendly forest spirits, including a gigantic gray animal called Totoro. Like all Miyazaki's films, *My Neighbor Totoro* is beautifully hand drawn and is filled with indelible, lush images and breathless scenes of racing, leaping, and flying. Every frame of the film is infused with Miyazaki's incredible imagination. "The cat bus in *My Neighbor Totoro* is a cat, and that's very cool," says *Toy Story* director John Lasseter, "But then the door opens and it's a live creature. . . . And the little mice that hang on to the cat bus are lights! It's just magnificent."[11]

Studio Ghibli's string of commercial and critical successes continued with 2001's *Spirited Away*, which many consider Miyazaki's masterpiece. Once again, the protagonist is a young girl who

Japanese animator Hayao Miyazaki is famous for creating strong female characters who interact with strange creatures and unusual people. Miyazaki's film, *Spirited Away* (2001), is considered by many critics to be his masterpiece.

accidentally wanders into the spirit realm, where she has bizarre adventures and meets many strange creatures. *Spirited Away* was so successful that it became the highest-grossing film in Japanese history. It also received the Academy Award for Best Animated Feature. Both the *New York Times* and the BBC have listed *Spirited Away* among the top five films of the twenty-first century.

Most of the audience who saw and enjoyed *Spirited Away* did not know anything about anime or manga. The film transcends such definitions, just as it defies description with its unique blend of the spiritual, the realistic, the fantastic, and the human. Academy Award–winning director Guillermo del Toro says, "There is a moment in which beauty moves you in a way that is impossible to describe. . . . It's an artistic act and you know nothing you will encounter in the natural world will be that pure. Miyazaki has that power."[12]

> "There is a moment in which beauty moves you in a way that is impossible to describe. . . . Miyazaki has that power."[12]
>
> —Guillermo del Toro, an Academy Award–winning director

The Digital Revolution

For many years Studio Ghibli has refused to allow its films to be distributed digitally or streamed. Miyazaki has said that he believes his films are best experienced on a big screen in a theater. But the internet has dramatically changed the way anime and manga are consumed by fans. Over the last ten years streaming services for anime have grown enormously. Big-name entertainment companies such as Netflix, Hulu, and Amazon are all building up their anime library as well as creating their own anime series. There are also popular services solely dedicated to anime, such as Crunchyroll, Funimation, VRV, and HIDIVE. Crunchyroll has over 2 million paid subscribers and 50 million registered users worldwide.

Manga is also going digital. In 2018 digital manga sales in Japan overtook print sales for the first time ever. Thanks to smartphones, many people can now read a wide variety of manga with a few clicks. There is serious concern about the fate of manga magazines as their role is being taken over by digital devices. "I am wondering how much longer the magazines can survive in their current form,"[13] says Shuhei Hosono, an editor at *Weekly Shonen Jump*, Japan's most famous manga magazine.

Even Studio Ghibli has finally decided to embrace the digital revolution. In late 2019 the studio announced that its acclaimed library of titles would be accessible to Americans on the HBO Max streaming service. Besides exposing its films to a much broader audience, streaming also provides more revenue. "Hayao Miyazaki is currently making a movie," Studio Ghibli cofounder Toshio Suzuki said in 2020, "but that takes a lot of time. And, of course, money."[14]

The future for anime and manga continues to look bright. Revenue is increasing, and movies such as *Demon Slayer: Mugen Train* are breaking box office records. Meanwhile, the growth of digital streaming means that nearly anyone in the world today can now enjoy these two uniquely Japanese art forms.

CHAPTER 2

The Universal Appeal of Anime and Manga

When Tesla and SpaceX founder Elon Musk tweeted about his love of anime in 2018, that statement quickly became his most popular tweet. Rapper Kanye West has said that his favorite movie is *Akira*. Pop star Ariana Grande sports a huge *Spirited Away* tattoo. And many professional basketball players have expressed their love for *Dragon Ball*.

Tech entrepreneurs, rappers, pop stars, and athletes are not the only ones who can relate to anime and manga. People of all ages and nationalities have embraced Japan's most popular cultural export. According to the anime streaming service Crunchyroll, the top ten countries using its site during the winter of 2020 were Uruguay, India, Peru, Colombia, the Philippines, Ecuador, Italy, El Salvador, Poland, and the Dominican Republic. Clearly, anime and manga have universal appeal, but why? What is it about the style, content, and messages of Japanese cartoons and comics that makes them so attractive to so many different types of people all over the world?

Identity and Belonging

For many young people, anime and manga give them one of the things they want most: a sense of identity. With identity comes purpose, and a sense of belonging. Many fans recall, later in life, how their favorite shows not only helped them figure out who they were but also how to accept themselves. "On the surface, it may have been a cartoon, but it had deeper themes that I could relate to," says anime blogger Lauren Orsini. "It was like none of the media that had been offered to me before. And at that time in my life where I didn't know where I belonged, I found my belonging there."[15]

Anime and manga were among the first media to address gender identity issues such as being transgender. The manga *Wandering Son*, which was first published in 2002, ran for eleven years. The series was created by Takako Shimura, who is primarily known for her manga works featuring LGBTQ topics. *Wandering Son* tells the story of two transgender friends; one is a trans boy and the other a trans girl. As they grow up, both try to come to terms with who they are while also navigating school, bullying, and relationships. In 2011 *Wandering Son* was turned into an internationally successful anime series.

Anime and manga often feature characters whose identities literally transform, often through magic. These characters seem ordinary on the outside, but they hide secret superpowers that can be activated by a command phrase. Sailor Moon is one of the most famous characters of this type. She transforms from a schoolgirl into an ancient lunar warrior called Sailor Moon from the Moon Kingdom. With the help of her guardians—Sailors Mercury, Mars, Jupiter, and Venus—she uses her superpowers to protect Earth from the forces of evil. *Sailor Moon* was massively popular during the 1990s and is often credited with introducing a whole new generation of fans—mostly young and female—to anime and manga. According to D.J. Kirkland, a Black gay comic book writer who cites *Sailor Moon* as the reason why he is an artist today, "I remember being 7 years-old and watching *Sailor Moon* for the first time and seeing her first transformation sequence and I was just mesmerized by it. Every time the Sailor Guardians held up their hands and got their nails done that matched the color of their outfits, I got my entire life."[16]

Escapism

One of the major appeals of anime and manga, for all fans, is escapism. Escapism is when people turn to entertainment or fantasy to distract themselves from reality. The great filmmaker Alfred Hitchcock once said, "I don't think many people want reality, whether it is in the theater or a film. It must look real, but it must *never* be real, because reality is something none of us can stand, at any time."[17]

Most everyone needs a break from reality sometimes. People all over the world are experiencing stress and anxiety—about the economy, climate change, the pandemic, and the rapid pace of technological and societal change. But Japanese people are especially stressed out. According to Japan's labor ministry, 60 percent of Japanese people are under constant stress, primarily due to overwork.

> "I don't think many people want reality . . . because reality is something none of us can stand, at any time."[17]
>
> —Alfred Hitchcock, film director

Perhaps that is why one of the most popular genres in anime and manga today is *isekai*, which means "another world." This is a type of fantasy where the main character is suddenly transported from the real world into a new, more exciting world. One of the most popular *isekai* is called *That Time I Got Reincarnated as a Slime*. It is about a thirty-seven-year-old corporate worker who gets murdered one night and wakes to find himself in a strange new world, reincarnated as a slime monster called Rimuru Tempest. Free from his stale past life, he uses his newfound powers to create a fairer and more just world. In 2019 the character Rimuru Tempest won "Best Protagonist" at the Crunchyroll Anime Awards.

People who spend a lot of time escaping into anime and manga are often called *otaku*. This term used to be derogatory and was used to describe people (usually men) who had an unhealthy preference for fantasy over reality. Today, though, the term simply refers to people who show their love for anime and manga by creating costumes, fan fiction, music videos, figures, and art. "(Otaku are) not just fans, but connoisseurs, critics, and authors themselves,"[18] says Tamaki Saitou, a Japanese psychologist and critic.

Sometimes, otaku are described as outcast loners. But that stereotype is completely wrong. In reality, being social is at the heart of otaku culture. Otaku gather as friends, in formal clubs, on message boards, at gaming arcades, and at giant conventions.

Some people, often called *otaku*, show their love of manga and anime by creating and dressing up in costumes.

According to one self-described otaku, "For me anime has proved the ultimate ice-breaker. Once coworkers discover we share an interest in the same anime, inhibitions fall and conversations flow."[19]

Unique Visuals

Back in 1963 Osamu Tezuka was the first to ever turn a manga into an animated television series—the iconic *Astro Boy*. But Tezuka had to overcome many challenges along the way. He had neither the time nor the money to make his animation look as fluid and realistic as a Disney cartoon. Disney used an animating technique called full animation, which is when every frame of film is individually hand drawn. Instead, Tezuka and his producers developed a new style called limited animation. Limited animation uses fewer frames of film to create an illusion of full motion. The result is choppier, less realistic, and not nearly as polished as Disney. But audiences loved it. Most anime artists today continue to use the limited animation style that Tezuka pioneered

Fan Service

The creators of anime and manga often present popular characters in ways that excite or titillate their fans. This is called fan service. A lot of fan service is sexual in nature. A popular female character might suddenly appear in a bikini, for example, even though it has nothing to do with the story. Fan service can be aimed at female audiences too, as when male characters go shirtless.

Fan service is not always sexual. It can include food, dancing, cute animals, or violence. A slow, lingering shot over the details of a spaceship or a robot is fan service. Anything that gives the viewer pleasure—but is not necessarily relevant to the plot—can be seen as fan service.

Fan service in anime and manga is often controversial in America. Many viewers see fan service as degrading to women. The Japanese, however, usually view it as harmless fun. They "do not take those sexual scenes too seriously," says Akiko Sugawa-Shimada, a professor at Yokohama National University.

Despite the controversy, most anime and manga fans enjoy fan service—up to a point. "Fanservice is like a spice," writes anime columnist Paul Jensen. "Just the right amount in the right recipe and it's fantastic, but too much overpowers the dish."

Quoted in Cecilia D'Anastasio, "Anime's Fan Service Can Be a Minefield," *Kotaku*, December 6, 2016. https://kotaku.com.

Paul Jensen, "Five Steps to Better Fanservice," *Anime News Network*, July 29, 2015. www.animenewsnetwork.com.

in *Astro Boy*, just as they continue to draw characters with Astro Boy's gigantic, expressive eyes. "From the start Tezuka . . . intentionally created *anime*, not *animation*,"[20] says Nobuyuki Tsugata, an associate professor of animation at Kyoto Seika University.

Fans love the distinctive look of anime precisely because it is *not* fluid and realistic. Instead, anime thrills viewers with stylized editing and imagery, bold still shots, striking poses, and dramatic effects. Limited animation is the perfect way to re-create manga because it is basically a series of still drawings with moving details. Some have even called anime "moving manga." In many ways, limited animation's lack of smooth, fluid movement became the style's greatest strength.

Limited animation also encourages the creation of imaginary worlds because artists spend more time working on the scenery and composition instead of movement. As a result, the settings in anime are often visually striking and richly detailed. This aesthetic, or style, is also shared by many video games. Not surprisingly, gaming is a popular genre in anime and manga. One of the most famous gaming anime is *Sword Art Online*, which tells the story of two gamers who are trapped in a virtual game world. To free themselves, they must complete each level of the ruthless game. The scenic landscapes in this virtual world are earthy and lush, and the sky exhibits a celestial and otherworldly appearance. "Young people brought up in a world of computers and video games are particularly open to [anime's] distinctive aesthetic,"[21] writes anime blogger Angel Qinglan Li.

Attractive Characters

One of these young anime fans is Chang Kim, a college student who lives in Japan. He has spent over $500 buying merchandise featuring the image of Asuna, his favorite character from *Sword Art Online*. "She's a good cook, good with kids, and she knows how to fend for herself. There's not much else I could ask for,"[22] says Kim of the character he calls his *waifu*. Fans use this word to describe anime characters on whom they have romantic crushes. The male version is *husbando*.

Although it might seem strange to have a crush on a two-dimensional character, it is really no different than having a crush on a pop star or film actor. Many anime fans with a waifu or husbando have healthy relationships with real people. "My girlfriend knows of my waifu, and she's fine with it because she has waifus of her own," says Kim. "Even if I get a wife in the future, Asuna will still always be my waifu."[23]

Why do so many anime and manga fans experience such strong, and often romantic, feelings toward the characters? One reason is limited animation. This animation technique favors character design over fluid movement. Since anime characters are somewhat static, artists must use visual clues to express personality, such as hairstyles, outfits, accessories, and poses.

Hair is especially important in anime. Loose, long hair on a girl is often associated with the popular kid, whereas hair that sticks out uncontrollably on a boy indicates a hot temper and aggression. Hairstyles come in all sorts of colors too: yellow, green, red, blue, and black. Each color offers clues to the character's personality. This kind of highly detailed and personalized design of anime characters makes them memorable and attractive to fans—and it also makes it easy to sell merchandise featuring their images.

Anime merchandise is big business, especially items that feature anime's most popular characters. The more attractive the character, the higher the sales. Merchandise ranges from figures and models to jewelry, clothes, hats, posters, bags, body pillows, coffee mugs, sneakers, and much more. Buying merchandise lets fans identify with their favorite characters. "You're trying to convey a message to others, showing that this is your fandom, and this is your ideal mate,"[24] says psychologist Robin Rosenberg.

Unusual Stories

Hollywood has tried to take advantage of the popularity of anime and manga by making their own, Americanized versions, but with little success. Perhaps the settings are simply too Japanese to Americanize, the visuals too unique, and the stories too weird to adapt for mainstream Western sensibilities.

How weird are some of the stories in anime and manga? In *Sekkou Boys*, a young woman becomes the manager of an up-and-coming boy idol group. The members of this group are a little unusual—they are Greco-Roman statues. Even though they have to be wheeled around on carts, their manager will do everything it takes to showcase their amazing talent. "This is probably one of the most bizarre shows that I have seen in my life,"

The 2020 Tokyo Summer Olympics

Before the 2020 Summer Olympics to be held in Toyko were canceled due to COVID-19, organizers had decided that popular anime and manga characters would be the official mascots for the games. The ambassadors included Astro Boy, Sailor Moon, Crayon Shin-chan, Monkey D. Luffy from *One Piece*, Naruto, Jibanyan from *Yo-kai Watch*, Son Goku from *Dragon Ball Super*, and Cure Miracle and Cure Magical from *Mahou Tsukai Pretty Cure*. Images of these characters were to appear on all official Olympic merchandise.

Anime has another connection with the canceled 2020 Tokyo Olympics. The groundbreaking 1988 anime film *Akira* takes place in Neo-Tokyo in the future year of 2019. At one point, the film shows a billboard advertising the 2020 Tokyo Olympics. It reads "147 Days Until the Games" and encourages citizens to support the event. But, curiously, under the message appears graffiti saying, "Just cancel it!" Although the movie does not address why the games should be canceled, "the story unfolds in a way that suggests a cancellation or a postponement [of the Olympics] is inevitable," says Kaichiro Morikawa, an expert on Japanese pop culture at Tokyo's Meiji University.

Quoted in Etienne Balmer, "World of Akira Foretells Olympics' Demise," *Asia Times*, March 28, 2020. https://asiatimes.com.

one confused anime fan said. "Talking Roman statues as your Japanese idols?!"[25]

Then there is the uncomfortable fact—for some Western audiences—that a lot of anime and manga is unapologetically sexual in nature. In *Kill La Kill*, Ryuko is a teenage girl hunting down her father's murderer. Her costume is so scanty and revealing that when one fan dressed like Ryuko for an anime convention, the police were called. But Ryuko's costume is more than just revealing—it is actually an alien being. By feeding on Ryuko's blood, her alien costume provides her with the strength she needs to wield her weapon, which is a giant pair of scissors. *Kill La Kill* was one of the most popular—and controversial—anime shows of 2014.

Strange and bizarre story lines are the rule in anime and manga, not the exception. Even the films of Hayao Miyazaki are filled with surreal and sometimes disturbing images. In an interview, he suggested that weird, fantastical stories can often reveal more about life than realistic ones can. "Lies must be layered upon lies to create a thoroughly believable fake world," he said. "The viewers know what they are seeing is fake, that it can't be reality, but at the same time they sense deep in their hearts that there is some sort of truth in the work."[26]

Anime and manga's universal appeal can also be explained by the huge variety of stories they tell. There are stories for children, teenagers, and adults. There are stories featuring adventure, romance, fantasy, sports, science fiction, and food. With so many options, manga and anime can appeal to just about anyone.

CHAPTER 3

Something for Everyone

While waiting for his train during the evening rush hour, a top executive for one of Tokyo's biggest companies walks over to a newsstand to buy the latest edition of *Big Comic for Men*. He heads to the nearest coffee shop and settles in to read the latest adventures of his favorite manga, *Golgo 13*, about a cold-blooded assassin for hire. He is not alone. Throughout the coffee shop, other businesspeople can be seen reading manga as well.

In Japan people of all ages and genders read manga. It is said there is a manga for everyone, and that is no joke. Subjects for manga include cooking, basketball, ghosts, fishing, ballet, medicine, politics, pop music, business, history, gambling, soccer, hairdressing, animals, acting, crime—the list goes on and on. The Japanese organize this huge variety of manga into five basic categories. These categories are not based on genre, or subject matter, but on the type of audience to which the manga is marketed.

Kodomomuke (Children Under Age Ten)

Literally meaning "directed at children," *kodomomuke* anime and manga are exactly that. They are cute, simple, and imaginative stories for young children that sometimes offer a moral lesson. *Astro Boy* is an early example of this type of story. But *Astro Boy*'s popularity—and profitability—pale in comparison to more contemporary kodomomuke titles such as *Pokémon* and *Hello Kitty*.

Known the world over, *Pokémon* revolves around cute little creatures that humans catch and train so they can fight each other. *Pokémon* began as a video game in 1996 and was later turned into a hit anime television series that ran for twenty seasons. *Pokémon*'s success is staggering. It is not only one of the most successful video games and television anime series of all time, but it is also the best-selling trading card game in history. In fact, *Pokémon* is currently the highest-grossing media franchise ever, with approximately $100 billion in revenue. *Hello Kitty*, another Japanese

Pokémon began as a video game in 1996 but has evolved into the highest-grossing media franchise of all time, with approximately $100 billion in revenue.

kodomomuke creation that was turned into an anime and manga series, is currently the second-highest-grossing media franchise in the world.

Shonen (Boys Ages Ten to Eighteen)

Shonen (meaning "few years") manga is aimed at a young male audience. These stories are filled with lots of action, adventure, and comedy and often deal with friendship and overcoming adversity. Shonen manga and anime such as *Dragon Ball* were among the first Japanese titles to be introduced to the Western world and are still the face of Japanese comics and cartoons for most Americans. Most of the best-selling shonen titles originated in the Japanese magazine *Weekly Shonen Jump*, the most popular manga magazine of all time. First published in 1968, it is also the longest running.

One of the most famous shonen titles is *One Piece*, which follows the adventures of Monkey D. Luffy, a teenage boy whose body becomes like rubber after he accidentally eats a Gum Gum Devil Fruit. Wearing his trademark straw hat, Luffy and his pirate crew sail all over the world in search of the priceless treasure called "One Piece." First appearing in *Weekly Shonen Jump* magazine in 1997, *One Piece* is the best-selling manga series in history. It was also turned into an anime in 1999, which aired nine hundred episodes. The international popularity of the series has made Monkey D. Luffy one of the world's most recognizable anime characters.

Shojo (Girls Ages Ten to Eighteen)

Shojo (meaning "young girl") manga is the female counterpart to shonen. Shojo stories are full of drama, emotion, and idealized romance. But they can also contain action, adventure, and comedy. In the United States, shojo manga has become increasingly popular as girls abandon traditional superhero comics. "Normal American comics like 'Superman' don't appeal to me that much," says fourteen-year-old Hilary Roberts. "They focus more on superheroes

Shojo (meaning "young girl") stories are full of drama, emotion, and idealized romance.

and fighting evil. Manga has more fantasy and it's more romantic. I think the art is prettier."[27]

One of the best-selling shojo series is the award-winning *Fruits Basket*. It tells the story of an orphaned teenage girl called Tohru who goes to live with a family hiding a big secret. She soon discovers that when family members are sick or are touched by someone of the opposite sex, they transform into the animals of the Chinese zodiac. As the series progresses, Tohru slowly uncovers the dark history behind this terrible curse and tries to heal the emotional wounds it has caused. Critic Jason Thompson describes *Fruits Basket* as "a fascinating manga, like a sweet, melancholy dream."[28] *Fruits Basket* was also turned into a successful anime series.

Just because a shojo title such as *Fruits Basket* is marketed to girls, it does not mean that boys cannot enjoy it, just as

"[*Fruits Basket* is] a fascinating manga, like a sweet, melancholy dream."[28]

—Jason Thompson, an anime and manga critic

girls can enjoy shonen titles like *One Piece*. It all boils down to personal taste. Many manga series, regardless of how they are marketed, are read and enjoyed by people that fall outside the targeted demographic.

Seinen (Men Ages Eighteen and Older)

Seinen anime and manga are targeted at adult men. Seinen is grittier and darker in tone, and features adult content such as sexual situations, graphic violence, and foul language. It takes a more realistic approach toward relationships and romance. Compared to titles for younger audiences, the topics and stories in the seinen category are much more diverse and can include comedy, politics, sports, horror, science fiction, mysteries, fantasy, history, and more.

Golgo 13 is an example of seinen manga. First published in 1968 *Golgo 13* is Japan's oldest manga series. It follows the adventures of a James Bond–like professional assassin for hire. This long-running series has been made into two live-action feature films, an anime film, an anime television series, and six video games.

Light Novels

Anime is often adapted from popular mangas, but increasingly anime is based upon another source—light novels. These books are usually short, easy to read, and often contain manga-style illustrations. Over the past decade, light novels have grown in popularity and are now another way for anime companies to promote their franchises.

In their constant search for new talent, publishers of light novels hold yearly writing contests, which attract thousands of submissions. The winner gets a cash prize and the publication of their novel. This is how the hugely popular *Sword Art Online* originated. Another way that publishers find new talent is through fan fiction, or amateur novels written by fans and posted online. If good enough, these amateur novels might be turned into a light novel, which could then become a manga, then an anime, and, if successful enough, a video game. This is what happened with *Re:Zero*, a story about a socially withdrawn young man who finds himself transported to another world on his way home from shopping. "Even after becoming so commercialized, one could say that light novels and their anime adaptations are created by the fans, for the fans," writes the Anime News Network's Kim Morrissy.

Kim Morrissy, "What's a Light Novel?," Anime News Network, October 19, 2016. www.animenewsnetwork.com.

Josei (Women Ages 18 and Older)

Josei anime and manga are aimed at adult women. Josei features realistic narratives exploring romantic and personal relationships, the work world, nightlife, sex, drug use, infidelity, and other aspects of adult life. Over the past decade, josei manga has greatly increased in popularity as a generation of girls who grew up reading shojo manga became women who wanted something more sophisticated and intellectually stimulating.

One of the most classic josei series is *Honey and Clover*, which follows a group of college friends in Toyko who live in the same apartment building. Together, they must deal with fickle relationships, unrequited love, and finding their place in the world. Filled with quirky humor and offbeat art, *Honey and Clover* has been adapted into a live-action movie, two television dramas, and two anime series.

The Many Genres of Anime and Manga

Manga is mainly categorized by audience first, then genre. For example, *Sailor Moon* is a shojo "magical girl" (subgenre) title. If you wanted to find something for a boy who likes adventure or horror, you would search for a "shonen adventure" or "shonen horror" manga. Popular genres include action, comedy, fantasy, science fiction, mystery, history, and romance—just to name a few. But there is also a huge number of subgenres, or genres within genres. Here are some examples of subgenres that have been growing in popularity recently.

Slice of Life

"Slice of life" stories tend to be slow and meditative, inviting readers or viewers to linger on the small moments in life that are often overlooked. There may or may not be any real plot or character development. With this kind of anime and manga, audiences can just sit back, relax, and not have to worry about following convoluted plots.

A good example of this subgenre is *Mushishi*, which follows the daily life of a man named Ginko who dedicates himself to keeping people protected from supernatural creatures called Mushi. Each episode is a complete story, and there are no villains or overarching plot to the season. Many fans love the ultra-soothing effect this show has on them, but it can also pack an emotional punch. "It is a series that is equal parts beautiful and haunting," writes critic Richard Eisenbeis, "often bringing more emotion in a 22-minute episode than most series can bring in their entire runs."[29]

Postapocalyptic

Postapocalyptic anime and manga have always been popular in Japan. Perhaps that is because much of the country was destroyed during World War II. Especially devastating were the two

The devastation wrought by the atomic bombing of Hiroshima and Nagasaki at the end of World War II haunts the Japanese psyche even today, and may explain the popularity of what is known as postapocalyptic anime and manga.

atomic bomb explosions in Hiroshima and Nagasaki. Visions of destruction, chaos, and survival continue to haunt the Japanese psyche even today. Most postapocalyptic anime and manga are set in a world that was nearly destroyed by atomic warfare, a natural disaster, an alien invasion, or a pandemic. Survivors must struggle to build a new society out of the ashes of the old world.

One of the most critically acclaimed postapocalyptic titles of the last decade is *Attack on Titan*. It is set in a world where humanity lives behind enormous walls that protect them from giant human-eating creatures called Titans. After a Titan kills the mother of a boy named Eren, he vows revenge and joins an elite group of soldiers dedicated to destroying the Titans. "The animation is spellbinding," writes Phelim O'Neill of *The Guardian*. "It's all wonderfully acrobatic and intense."[30]

Sports

Even for people who do not care about sports, stories that focus on athletes can thrill and inspire as they show people working hard to become the best they can be. Character development plays a huge role in sports stories; players must learn to focus, sacrifice, deal with failure, and fully commit to the game. This genre features many kinds of sports, including soccer, basketball, baseball, tennis, boxing, biking, swimming, volleyball, surfing, table tennis, diving, and more.

One of the most popular and highly acclaimed sports series of recent years is *Yuri on Ice*. It is about an anxious, depressed figure skater named Yuri whose fortunes turn around when his idol, Victor Nikiforov, agrees to coach him. Victor inspires Yuri's love for skating—and for Victor himself. "Yuri on Ice, in depicting a sincere and uncomplicated engagement between two dudes, is unprecedented in anime,"[31] writes Gabriella Ekens at the Anime News Network. Many professional figure skaters are fans of *Yuri on Ice*, and some even skated to music from the show at the 2018 Winter Olympics in South Korea.

"*Yuri on Ice*, in depicting a sincere and uncomplicated engagement between two dudes, is unprecedented in anime."[31]

—Gabriella Ekens, a writer at the Anime News Network

Mecha

Mecha (short for "mechanical") or "robot anime" is one of the oldest genres in anime and manga, dating all the way back to *Astro Boy*. This genre features robots of all sorts, from humanoid robots like Astro Boy to giant robots as big as skyscrapers. Mecha reached the height of its popularity in Japan during the 1970s and 1980s, with massively popular shows such as *Gundam*. Mecha continues to have a rabid fan base, and the genre is one that has been consistently popular over the years.

One of the most acclaimed mecha anime of the twenty-first century is *Gurren Lagann*. It is set in the future when Earth is ruled by a king called Lordgenome, who forces humanity to live underground. After two teenagers discover a key that activates a robot known as Lagann, they travel to the earth's surface and start fighting against Lordgenome's forces. Tim Jones of THEM Anime Reviews writes that *Gurren Lagann* "is chock full of action, comedy, drama, adventure, and sci-fi elements, managing to even entertain a person who couldn't care less about mecha in the process."[32]

Food

Japan boasts one of the best food cultures in the world, so it is no surprise that food is a popular subject for anime and manga. These stories take place in restaurants, cafés, cooking schools, and home kitchens. Some feature step-by-step recipes and techniques, and others revolve around intense cooking or baking competitions. The one thing all these stories have in common is that they celebrate food and eating in a positive, joyous way.

Food Wars! is probably the most famous cooking anime because it combines the excitement of a shonen action series with comedy, competition, and self-improvement. The plot follows a teenage boy named Soma, who has enrolled at an elite culinary school famous for its high stakes cooking showdowns between students. The show appeals to all age groups, but why do teenagers like it so much? According to cartoonist Deb Aoki, "When Soma cooks something really delicious, people put it in their mouths and they are so overcome with ecstasy that their clothes explode off. If the food is not good enough, then the guy still has his clothes on."[33]

A lot of anime and manga does not fit neatly into a single category or genre. Shonen stories are often enjoyed by girls as well as boys. Stories that are marketed as shojo might just as easily be marketed as josei. And many stories include more than one genre. For example, there are postapocalyptic slice-of-life stories. Fans will often argue about how to categorize their favorite shows. One thing is certain, though: anime and manga feature a truly endless variety of story lines, characters, and settings.

CHAPTER 4

Essential Anime and Manga

Until the mid-1990s most people, including the Japanese, viewed televised anime as simplistic entertainment for children. Shows were usually about robots fighting, but little else. That changed when *Neon Genesis Evangelion* aired in October 1995.

Set in the future, *Neon Genesis Evangelion* revolves around an introverted teenage boy who helps save Earth from destruction by bonding with a giant humanoid robot of near godlike power called an Evangelion. On the surface, *Neon Genesis Evangelion* was about robots fighting, but the show also delved deeply into serious issues, including depression, loneliness, trauma, and the difficulty of finding personal meaning in a time of apocalypse.

Before *Neon Genesis Evangelion*, anime shows tended to run for hundreds of episodes and were usually based on popular manga that had broad, mainstream appeal. *Neon Genesis Evangelion* was an original series, ran for only twenty-six episodes, and was often difficult to comprehend, especially the controversial final two episodes. These episodes did not feature any fighting at all but instead consisted of forty minutes of introspective dialogue between the characters. Despite the controversy, the series was hugely popular and attracted many new fans to anime.

The success of *Neon Genesis Evangelion* spawned a new kind of anime that was more serious, artistic, adult oriented, and sometimes just plain weird. The artistic and technical innovations pioneered by *Neon Genesis Evangelion* can be seen in many of the most important and influential anime titles of the past twenty-five years.

The televised anime series *Neon Genesis Evangelion* revolves around an introverted teenage boy (center), who bonds with a gigantic humanoid robot that has near godlike powers.

Ghost in the Shell

In addition to *Neon Genesis Evangelion*, the year 1995 also saw the premiere of the anime film *Ghost in the Shell*. This film is a perfect example of cyberpunk, which is a subgenre of science fiction that is set in a dystopian, high-tech future often involving characters who are cyborgs—part human, part machine. In *Ghost in the Shell* a cyborg named Major Motoko Kusanagi finds herself caught up in a tangled web of intrigue and espionage as she searches for a powerful hacker called the Puppet Master. Critic Noel Murray calls *Ghost in the Shell* "an ultra-violent, rocket-paced film . . . but it's a poetic one, too."[34] *Ghost in the Shell* was the first anime to reach number one on Billboard's video best-seller list, and it was also a major inspiration for the Matrix movies. James Cameron, the director of *Avatar*, has described *Ghost in the Shell* as "a stunning work of speculative fiction . . . the first to reach a level of literary excellence."[35]

"[*Ghost in the Shell* is] a stunning work of speculative fiction . . . the first to reach a level of literary excellence."[35]

—James Cameron, film director

Death Note

The 2015 psychological thriller *Death Note* is about a student named Light who finds a magical notebook. Whenever Light writes someone's name in the notebook, that person dies. With his new godlike power, Light decides to kill criminals one by one to help make a better world. But the police see things differently, and they enlist the help of an eccentric detective named L to discover the identity of this mysterious new serial killer. "One of the greatest animes of all time," writes Maya Phillips in *Vulture*. She says it "addresses questions about morality, justice, and capital punishment. All this, plus beautiful animation and well-written dialogue and plot, makes *Death Note* the cream of the animated crop."[36]

Death Note has created quite a bit of controversy. In schools around the world, students have been disciplined and suspended for keeping replica *Death Note* notebooks in which they have written down the names of students and teachers they do not like. *Death Note* has been banned in China, and attempts to ban it have occurred in the United States.

Your Name

The highest-grossing animated film of all time, *Your Name*, is a 2016 romantic fantasy about a teenage girl and boy who swap bodies in their dreams. They leave cell phone messages for each and gradually begin to fall in love even though they have never met. *Your Name* was directed by Makoto Shinkai, whom many have compared to Hayao Miyazaki.

Critics have especially praised the incredible artwork and attention to detail in *Your Name*. Every background scene and

Whitewashing Controversies

Both *Death Note* and *Ghost in the Shell* have been made into poorly reviewed live-action American movies, but they have received attention for an issue that has nothing to do with their quality. Both films have been accused of "whitewashing," which is when white actors are cast as characters that were originally a different race (in this case, Asian).

When leading actress Scarlett Johansson was cast as the cyborg Major Motoko Kusanagi (simply called "Major" in the film) in *Ghost in the Shell*, fans launched a petition for the role to be recast: "The original film is set in Japan, and the major cast members are Japanese. So why would the American remake star a white actress?" Similar accusations of whitewashing arose when white actor Nat Wolff was cast to play the lead in *Death Note*.

However, some defend the casting, arguing that these films are American remakes. *Death Note*, for example, is set in the city of Seattle. *Death Note* producer Masi Oka says the character was not written to be Asian. "The whole idea of whitewashing is putting white people in roles that were meant to be a different race. But this wasn't specifically a racially bound story, because it was set in America."

Quoted in Eliza Berman, "A Comprehensive Guide to the *Ghost in the Shell* Controversy," *Time*, March 29, 2017. https://time.com.

Quoted in Katie Van Syckle, "*Death Note* Director Adam Wingard Is Ready to Talk About Whitewashing," *Vulture*, August 18, 2017. www.vulture.com.

Your Name (2016), the highest-grossing animated film of all time, is a romantic fantasy about a teenage boy and girl who swap bodies in their dreams.

building can be identified. In fact, tours to visit the places depicted in the film have become popular in Japan. "Beautifully animated (we're talking Studio Ghibli standards here), *Your Name* captures that sensation of waking up from a dream you wish lasted longer,"[37] writes critic Kristen Yoonsoo Kim in *Brooklyn Magazine*.

Fullmetal Alchemist

The popular manga and anime series *Fullmetal Alchemist* follows the adventures of two brothers named Edward and Alphonse Elric. After severely injuring themselves in a failed attempt to bring their dead mother back to life using alchemy, they search for the mythical philosopher's stone in the hope of restoring their bodies. *Fullmetal Alchemist* has been praised for its flawed, realistic characters, imaginative story line, and steampunk visuals. Steampunk is a subgenre of science fiction and is set in the future, but its style and technology harken back to the steam-powered machinery of nineteenth-century Victorian England.

Called "one of the classic shonen manga series"[38] of the 2000s by critic Jason Thompson of the Anime News Network, the manga version of *Fullmetal Alchemist* has been adapted twice into anime series. The story of the first anime, also titled *Fullmetal Alchemist*, ran ahead of the ongoing manga series and had to continue with an original story line that drastically diverged from the direction the manga ended up taking. The second, later version, called *Fullmetal Alchemist Brotherhood*, is a faithful adaptation of the full manga series.

Revolutionary Girl Utena

Revolutionary Girl Utena is one of the rare series with LGBTQ main characters. This shojo story is about a teenage girl named Utena who wants to be a prince. She attends a high school where students duel with swords to try to win the hand of a mysterious girl who has the power to revolutionize the world. Imaginative, complex, bizarre, and highly symbolic, the story line of *Revolutionary Girl Utena* leaves a lot open to interpretation.

Created by many of the same people who made *Sailor Moon*, *Revolutionary Girl Utena* began as a manga in 1996 and was turned into an anime series in 1997. Although it is considered to be a classic shojo that redefined the genre, *Revolutionary Girl Utena* explores dark topics that some people might find uncomfortable, including domestic abuse, sexual assault, and suicide. This is "a story about gender, it's a story about sexuality," writes Caitlin Donovan of the website the Mary Sue. "While *Revolutionary Girl Utena* can be compared to many things, there is nothing quite like it and probably never will be."[39]

"While *Revolutionary Girl Utena* can be compared to many things, there is nothing quite like it and probably never will be."[39]

—Caitlin Donovan, an anime critic and journalist

Cowboy Bebop

First televised in 1998 the anime series *Cowboy Bebop* was a sensation not only in Japan but also in the United States, where it is credited with introducing anime to a whole new audience of

The *Cowboy Bebop* Soundtrack

The soundtrack for *Cowboy Bebop* is one of the most famous and ambitious original anime scores ever composed. Like the show itself, the soundtrack moves effortlessly through a variety of genres. The result is a classic jazz soundtrack full of energetic bebop songs, sultry mood pieces, and operatic bombast. The music was composed by Yoko Kanno and performed by a band she put together for the show called the Seatbelts. Kanno says, "I chose to create such music believing that people's emotions in their everyday life would be the same in the future, even in outer space."

Cowboy Bebop director Shinichiro Watanabe says that working with Kanno was an unusual experience. "She does not compose music exactly the way I tell her to," he said. Kanno would often go off on her own and compose new music without being asked to do so. But this music was so good that it inspired Watanabe to create new scenes. These scenes would then give Kanno new ideas, and she would compose even more music. "It was a game of catch between the two of us in developing the music and creating the TV series *Cowboy Bebop*," says Watanabe.

Quoted in Gunseli Yalcinkaya, "*Cowboy Bebop* Composer Yoko Kanno Reinvented What Anime Scores Could Be," Dazed, December 3, 2020. www.dazeddigital.com.

Quoted in Todd DuBois, "Otakon 2013: Press Conference and Public Q&A with Director Shinichiro Watanabe," Anime Superhero, August 21, 2013. https://animesuperhero.com.

Western viewers. Many critics have called *Cowboy Bebop* a masterpiece and often cite it as one of the greatest, if not the greatest, anime titles of all time.

Based on an original script, *Cowboy Bebop* follows a crew of bounty hunters as they travel through a galaxy of lawlessness in the spaceship *Bebop*. The show is a mash-up of many different genres, including science fiction, comedy, action, cyberpunk, martial arts, westerns, and stylish crime movies of the 1940s. Every aspect of *Cowboy Bebop* has been singled out for praise, from the complex characters whose dark pasts are revealed as the plot progresses to the jazz-heavy soundtrack and pop art opening credits. "It changed anime," says Cartoon Network producer Sean Akins. "I think it redefined cool within animation, not only in Japan but in the States."[40]

Naruto

One of the world's most popular manga and anime series, *Naruto* is a classic shonen title full of action, adventure, comedy, and positive messages about the power of hard work, perseverance, and friendship. Naruto is a young ninja from the Hidden Leaf Village. His dream is to gain the respect and recognition of his peers and to become the village *Hokage*, the most powerful ninja who leads the village.

First appearing in 1999 the *Naruto* manga ran for fifteen years and is the fourth-best-selling manga series in history. In 2002 the manga was adapted as an anime series and ran for 220 episodes. The sequel, *Naruto: Shippuden*, ran for a whopping 500 episodes. "*Naruto* just has that special something that allows it to endure in a constantly shifting media landscape, appealing to readers and viewers time and time again,"[41] writes Morgana Santilli on the Looper website.

Ouran High School Host Club

Girls who look like boys; boys who look like girls; boys who look like girls in love with girls who look like boys. It sounds confusing, but it is just an average episode of the screwball romantic comedy *Ouran High School Host Club*, a famous shojo manga and anime series from the early 2000s.

Set in a school for rich kids, the story begins when a poor female student breaks an expensive vase and is forced to repay the debt by working at the school's secret all-male club—as a boy! But as she is getting used to her new job—flirting with female clients—she starts forming romantic relationships with some of the club's extremely wealthy and handsome members.

A parody of the clichés and stereotypes that are often found in shojo manga and anime, *Ouran High School Host Club* has been praised for its charm, wit, humor, and soundtrack. The anime was so popular that it was made into a live-action film and television series. *Ouran High School Host Club* is a "landmark series [that is] still clever and heartfelt enough to pull in new fans,"[42] writes Rose Bridges at the Anime News Network.

JoJo's Bizarre Adventure

An explosive mix of fast-paced absurdity, *JoJo's Bizarre Adventure* is a groundbreaking, one-of-a-kind experience. The series is divided into eight separate stories, each following a member of the Joestar family as they wield their special powers against supernatural villains down through the generations. The manga version of *JoJo's Bizarre Adventure* first appeared in 1983 and is still going strong—making it one of the longest-running manga series in history. An anime version started airing in 2012.

Known for its striking artwork, frequent references to Western fashion and popular music, and highly creative fight scenes, *JoJo's Bizarre Adventure* is hard to categorize. It was first published as a shonen series but was later switched over to a seinen magazine. There is simply nothing else that compares to its playfully eccentric style; melodramatic story line; and beautiful, weird characters, who strut around in colorful, avant-garde outfits while striking dramatic poses. "*JoJo's Bizarre Adventure* is one of the most outrageous and joyous series I have ever watched," writes Gita Jackson on the Kotaku website. "You owe it to yourself to experience it."[43]

Nana

Female friendship, cool fashions, and amazing artwork have helped make *Nana* a best-selling manga and anime series. First appearing in 2000, the manga follows two young women, both of whom are named Nana. One is a naive, small-town girl, and the other is a tattooed, chain-smoking rock singer. After meeting on a train to Tokyo, they become roommates, each helping the other deal with boyfriends, jobs, and family.

The author of *Nana*, Ai Yazawa, has said her goal in writing the series was to help women make it through their difficult twenties. "Realizing that you are not alone with your pain and self-doubt can be a source of comfort,"[44] she said. Unfortunately, Yazawa became ill in 2009 and has yet to finish the series.

In addition to the anime series, *Nana* has also inspired two live-action films, a video game, and a tribute album. "*Nana* is a beautifully-drawn series that is filled with heartfelt drama, big city glamor, fabulous fashion, rock and roll sass and many unexpected twists," writes Deb Aoki on the LiveAbout website. "It's the kind of shojo series that sucks you in and won't let you go, volume after volume."[45]

FLCL

FLCL is the story of a twelve-year-old suburban boy who, after getting hit in the head by a guitar swung by an alien girl, must then deal with robots popping out of his wound. After that things get weird. "Difficulty in comprehension should not be an important factor in *FLCL*,"[46] says director Kazuya Tsurumaki.

FLCL, otherwise known as *Fooly Cooly*, is unique. The original series first appeared in 2000 and was only six episodes long, but it quickly developed a cult following. Two more seasons were added in 2016. With its manic editing, fast-paced soundtrack, and shifting animation styles, *FLCL* often appears to be more music video than anime, but beneath all the noise is a heartfelt coming-of-age story. "Incredibly innovative, immensely endearing, and above all else blissfully entertaining, *FLCL* is in a class by itself. It is one of the very few works of genius in recent anime history,"[47] writes Mike Crandol on the Anime News Network.

CHAPTER 5

The Future of Anime and Manga

Growing up in America, Henry Thurlow watched cartoons on television like any other kid. But it was not until he discovered anime that he developed a passion for drawing. After college, Thurlow worked in New York as an animator for web games, children's shows, and music videos, but he found much of the work unfulfilling. So, he decided to move to Japan to make anime.

It took four years of hard work, but he finally got his break and became one of the few Americans working in the anime industry in Japan. "The projects are amazing and there's a sense of pride that you're among (or at least surrounded by) the best of the best," says Thurlow. "Unfortunately, as far as 'good things about the anime industry' go, that's about it . . . . They don't pay you even remotely minimum wage, they overwork you to the point where people are vomiting at work and having to go to the hospital for medicine." Thurlow himself ended up in the hospital three times suffering from illness and exhaustion. Nevertheless, he continues to work in the industry, saying, "everything about my life is utterly horrible, however the artist in me is completely satisfied."[48]

The Dark Side of Japanese Animation

In many ways, the future of anime and manga is incredibly bright. Thanks to streaming services like Netflix, Hulu, Crunchyroll, and Funimation, anime is now spreading all over the world, creating legions of new fans and bringing in billions of dollars in revenue.

But there is a dark side to this success. Salaries and working conditions for most animators in Japan are terrible. According to the Japanese Animation Creators Association, animators in their twenties earn an average of $10,000 per year, animators in their thirties earn around $19,000 per year, and animators in their forties and fifties earn $31,000 per year. But low pay is only part of the problem. Overwork is another, and perhaps more serious, issue.

Working long hours without a break is common throughout Japanese society. There is even a word for it—*karoshi*—which translates to "death from overwork." The animation industry in

Webtoons

Comics in South Korea are known as *manhwa*. Back in the early 2000s, *manhwa* became almost exclusively digital, which led to them being called "webtoons." Webtoons are read vertically, from top to bottom. This format is perfect for smartphones and other digital devices. Many also feature music and animation to create a mixed-media experience.

Webtoon is the also the name of a South Korean company that publishes webtoons through an app. Most of the content is free for users. Because of its low cost and ease of use, this app has become one of the most popular in the world. There are over 6 million daily users, making Webtoon one of the largest and most successful comic publishing companies in the world. It has even partnered with Crunchyroll, which is now producing animated shows based on popular webtoons, such as *Tower of God* and *The God of High School*.

Some think webtoons represent the future for Japan's manga industry. "Japanese publishers are now at a stage where they can't overlook the need for going digital and overseas. . . . Webtoons, I think, are the most reasonable way forward," says one manga editor.

Quoted in Tomohiro Osaki, "South Korea's Booming 'Webtoons' Put Japan's Print Manga on Notice," *Japan Times*, May 5, 2019. www.japantimes.co.jp.

Japan is notorious for its long hours, tight deadlines, and demanding work schedules. It is common for animators to fall asleep at their desks or work while sick. Thomas Romain, a French animator living in Tokyo, says, "I've seen people going home only once per week, or working 35 hours in a row . . . [or] camping in a corner of the studio, sleeping in sleeping bags until the production was finished."[49]

Animators in Japan put up with such terrible conditions because they love what they do. For many of them working in the anime industry is a dream come true. "When you see your show being broadcast, and you know you worked on it, it's the greatest feeling ever,"[50] says one animator. But increasingly, the prospect of low pay and bad working conditions are scaring off young animators, and the industry is beginning to suffer for it. "Perhaps the biggest problem in the Japanese animation industry is that there are no more young animators,"[51] warns award-winning director Keiichi Hara.

"Perhaps the biggest problem in the Japanese animation industry is that there are no more young animators."[51]

—Keiichi Hara, director

A Broken System

A lot of the problems in the anime and manga industry can be traced back to Osamu Tezuka, the creator of *Astro Boy*. During the early 1960s television networks were reluctant to take a chance on an animated cartoon series, so Tezuka was forced to sell his show to them cheaply. But he made up his financial losses by selling *Astro Boy* toys, figures, and other merchandise. Ultimately, he made money this way. Because this system worked for Tezuka, it remains in place today.

This system might still work if animation were as simple and inexpensive to make as it was in Tezuka's day, but anime today is far more detailed and costly. It can take an army of animators working around the clock to complete a single episode. As a result, anime is rarely profitable. It is not uncommon for animation studios to go out of business, even if they pay their animators next to nothing while overworking them.

This seems incredible when considering that the anime and manga industry generates over $20 billion of revenue per year. If the studios are not making a profit, then who is? Perhaps the biggest piece of the revenue pie goes to companies that manufacture toys, figures, and other merchandise that is so popular among fans. Television networks that broadcast anime also make a lot of money. Finally, Western companies like Netflix, Hulu, and other streaming services make a substantial profit because they are able to license anime shows for dirt-cheap prices, thanks to the precedent set long ago by Tezuka and *Astro Boy*. "It's a pyramid structure, where many at the bottom work to support a few at the top. I don't see a bright future,"[52] says Shingo Adachi, an animator who worked on *Sword Art Online*.

Resisting Change

Ideas for improving the lives of animators in Japan have been debated by industry insiders. Some believe that animators need to organize and form unions that will fight for better pay and working

Although animators in Japan work long hours for low pay, many say that working in the anime industry is a dream come true.

conditions. The problem is that animation studios often rely on freelance artists. Freelancers are not considered employees, so the labor laws do not apply to them. This means the studios can enforce grueling deadlines while saving money by not providing benefits. To be fair to the studios, most of them do not have the money to properly pay their animators. Increasing salaries would cause many studios to go bankrupt.

"It's a pyramid structure, where many at the bottom work to support a few at the top. I don't see a bright future."[52]

—Shingo Adachi, animator

Ultimately the only way to make things fairer and more equitable is to "radically reform the profit structure of the entire industry,"[53] according to a 2016 report by Teikoku Databank, a leading Japanese financial research group. But this is a daunting challenge on many levels. For one thing, the people making all the money—the streaming services, television networks, and merchandising companies—are not motivated to change the system, especially as revenue continues to rise. In addition Japanese culture tends to resist change. After all, the animation industry is still using the limited animation technique and business model pioneered by the creator of *Astro Boy* more than half a century ago. Change is even harder to bring about because of a business culture in Japan that encourages people to agree to work under impossible conditions. "This is a country that believes in . . . sucking it up and getting through it. That . . . is an absolute brake on change,"[54] says Brad Glosserman, the author of *Peak Japan: The End of Great Ambitions*.

Some people believe the Japanese government should do more to improve animators' lives by offering financial support. After all, they argue, anime and manga are now an important part of Japan's cultural identity. "Japanese pop culture—anime, manga, even characters like Hello Kitty . . . those things are unique,"[55] says Tetsu Fujimura, an executive film producer. In the past, he adds, Japanese parents used to scold their kids for wasting so

Some observers argue that because anime and manga characters such as Hello Kitty have become part of Japan's cultural identity, the Japanese government should offer financial support to improve animators' lives.

much time reading manga or watching anime. Now Japan feels a deep sense of pride in these art forms that are beloved by so many around the world.

Change Is Coming

Although the profit structure of the anime and manga industries seems unlikely to be reformed anytime soon, change is coming nonetheless—in the form of technology. "The future is digital in Japan; there's no avoiding the situation," says Thurlow. "In five to ten years, everybody will be digital."[56]

But even here there is considerable resistance in the industry. Many Japanese artists prefer to stick to the old-fashioned hand-drawn style. After all, this is what gives anime and manga its distinct personality. Technology, they believe, will limit their creativity and compromise the integrity of their art. After watching a clip of animation made primarily with artificial intelligence technology, seventy-five-year-old Hayao Miyazaki said, "I would never wish to incorporate this technology into my work at all. I strongly feel that this is an insult to life itself. . . . We humans are losing faith in ourselves."[57]

But as anime's popularity continues to grow around the world, studios in Japan are having trouble keeping up with the demand. There is more work to be done but fewer qualified artists willing to put up with low pay and bad working conditions. "The problem with anime is that it just takes way too long to make," says one animator. "It's extremely meticulous."[58] To make matters worse, the world is now transitioning to higher-resolution televisions and streaming devices. In order not to appear fuzzy, anime needs to be drawn even more precisely than ever before—which takes even *more* time and effort.

Technology is now advanced enough to offer solutions to these problems. For example, a Tokyo-based company called RADIUS5 has recently developed an artificial intelligence program that takes rough hand drawings and turns them into richly detailed images. What used to be a lengthy process can now be done quickly and with far fewer staff. Most importantly, the artistic personality of the images remains intact.

Artificial intelligence programs can also help solve problems in the manga industry. Manga, like anime, is increasingly in demand throughout the world. But translating manga into so many different languages is time-consuming and expensive. And translation can be tricky because manga often features unusual typographical characters, street slang, and culturally unique wordplay. To help speed up

> "The future is digital in Japan; there's no avoiding the situation."[56]
>
> —Henry Thurlow, animator

> "The problem with anime is that it just takes way too long to make. It's extremely meticulous."[58]
>
> —Zakoani, animator

the translation process, a company called Mantra developed an artificial intelligence program that has been able to study and learn the many linguistic peculiarities found in manga. This enables the program to translate manga into a wide variety of languages quickly and accurately, although humans are still needed to check the work for mistakes.

Digitally Assisted Animation

Some animation studios are already using technology in innovative, creative ways. One of them is called Science SARU, which translates to "Science Monkey." This studio combines traditional hand-drawn animation with digital animation to create what they call digitally assisted animation.

Here is how it works: A skilled animator draws the most important frames of animation by hand. These are called "keyframes." There are maybe two or three keyframes per second, which might seem like a lot, but it is not enough to create the illusion of movement. You need more frames to go in between the keyframes. These frames are called "in-betweens."

At a traditional anime studio, less-skilled animators draw the in-betweens. These are usually freelancers who get paid around two dollars a drawing. It can take more than an hour to produce a drawing. But at Science SARU, computer software produces the in-betweens, creating smooth, fluid motion. The process saves an immense amount of time and human labor. This is just one way that studios are using technology to create a new form of anime while keeping the personality and spirit of traditional animation.

But are anime fans and critics ready to fully embrace digitally assisted animation? It appears so. In 2018 Netflix released an anime series called *Devilman Crybaby*, which was animated by Science SARU. The plot revolves around a man who merges with a demon in order to kill other demons. One critic wrote "a simultaneous punch to the face and gut. The gore and extremely upset-

Breaking Barriers

D'Art Shtajio is an anime studio founded in 2016 by Henry Thurlow and Arthell and Darnell Isom, twin brothers who are African American. It is not only the first Black-owned studio in Japan but also the first American studio. Some of the popular shows they have worked on include *One Piece*, *Attack on Titan*, and *Tokyo Ghoul*.

D'Art Shtajio is part of a new generation of animators who want to diversify the industry on- and off-screen. "We don't approach things thinking that we're going to be political activists, but we choose characters that would be cool to represent right at this moment," says Arthell, the studio's art director.

In high school, Arthell watched *Ghost in the Shell* every day for a year, which made him realize he needed to become an artist. After studying art in Japan, he worked as an intern for Hiromasa Ogura, the film's legendary art director, an experience he describes as "life-changing." Looking forward, Arthell would like to work on more projects involving underrepresented voices. "There's not a lot of Black, or generally diverse, characters in anime yet, and hearing these stories makes us want to do something with them."

Quoted in Gunseli Yalcinkaya, "Meet the Creator Behind the First Major Black-Owned Anime Studio," Dazed, August 3, 2020. www.dazeddigital.com.

ting dramatic turns aren't for the weak of heart, but that doesn't make it any less good."[59]

Fans and critics loved the quality of the animation in *Devilman Crybaby*. In fact, the show was awarded Anime of the Year at the Crunchyroll Anime Awards, and many critics called it one of the best Japanese animated series of the decade. Science SARU cofounder Eunyoung Choi says she is thrilled by the overwhelmingly positive response to *Devilman Crybaby*: "I wanted to take on the challenge of creating high-quality animation digitally in Japan, where many didn't believe it could work with the time-honored traditional ways. Now that it's done, I hope that we've added a new chapter to the traditions that came before and inspired us."[60]

SOURCE NOTES

Introduction: Setting New Records

1. Quoted in *Japan Times*, "'Demon Slayer' Fastest Movie to Rake In ¥10 Billion in Japan," October 26, 2020. www.japan times.co.jp.
2. Quoted in Julian Ryall, "Japan's 'Demon Slayer' Anime Trumps 'Spirited Away' at Box Office amid Covid-19 Pandemic," *South China Morning Post*, October 27, 2020. www .scmp.com.
3. Quoted in Ryall, "Japan's 'Demon Slayer' Anime Trumps 'Spirited Away' at Box Office amid Covid-19 Pandemic."
4. Quoted in Erika Salemme, "The Rising Popularity of Anime," *Sandbox News*, October 29, 2019. https://sandbox.sp college.edu.
5. Quoted in Maxwell Williams, "How Netflix and Other Streaming Services Are Doubling Down on Anime," *Variety*, July 29, 2019. https://variety.com.
6. Quoted in Williams, "How Netflix and Other Streaming Services Are Doubling Down on Anime."

Chapter 1: Origin Story

7. Tim Clark, "Hokusai: The Father of Manga?," *British Museum* (blog), May 10, 2019. https://blog.britishmuseum.org.
8. Quoted in Sheri Le and Will Dodds, "Manga: Evolution," Right Stuf Anime. www.rightstufanime.com.
9. Craig Elvy, "No Other Anime Will Ever Emulate *Dragon Ball*'s Success," Screen Rant, February 13, 2020. https://screen rant.com.
10. Stephen Hunter, "Extraordinary Animation, Powerful Vision Breathe Life into 'Akira's' Violent Future," *Baltimore Sun*, September 13, 1990. www.baltimoresun.com.
11. Quoted in Jennifer Wolfe, "John Lasseter Pays Tribute to Hayao Miyazaki at Tokyo Film Festival," Animation World Network, October 27, 2014. www.awn.com.

12. Quoted in Manohla Dargis and A.O. Scott, "The Best 25 Films of the 21st Century So Far," *New York Times*, June 9, 2017. www.nytimes.com.

13. Quoted in Kazuaki Nagata, "As Manga Goes Digital via Smartphone Apps, Do Paper Comics Still Have a Place?," *Japan Times*, August 2, 2017. www.japantimes.co.jp.

14. Quoted in Nick Romano, "Streaming, More Miyazaki, and Reminiscence: How Studio Ghibli Is Adapting for the Future," *Entertainment Weekly*, May 20, 2020. https://ew.com.

Chapter 2: The Universal Appeal of Anime and Manga

15. Quoted in Kami Nomi, "5 Reasons Why People Love Anime: Interview with Industry Professionals," MyAnimeList, February 14, 2016. https://myanimelist.net.

16. Quoted in Ryan Khosravi, "'Sailor Moon' and the Queer History of Anime Transformations," Digg, December 19, 2018. https://digg.com.

17. Quoted in George Edelman, "Get Alfred Hitchcock's Advice, in His Own Words," No Film School, August 13, 2020. https://nofilmschool.com.

18. Quoted in Rich, "How I Learned to Stop Worrying and Love Being Otaku," Tofugu, June 6, 2016. www.tofugu.com.

19. Rich, "How I Learned to Stop Worrying and Love Being Otaku."

20. Quoted in Rich, "Anime's Great Deception—the Difference Between Anime and Cartoons," Tofugu, July 1, 2015. www.tofugu.com.

21. Angel Qinglan Li, "The Appeal of Japanese Anime," *New Cultural Analyst* (blog), April 9, 2015. https://newculturalanalyst.wordpress.com.

22. Quoted in Lauren Orsini, "Why Adults Fall in Love with (and Spend Big Money on) Cartoon Characters," *Forbes*, June 12, 2015. www.forbes.com.

23. Quoted in Orsini, "Why Adults Fall in Love with (and Spend Big Money on) Cartoon Characters."

24,. Quoted in Orsini, "Why Adults Fall in Love with (and Spend Big Money on) Cartoon Characters."

25. Quoted in Phil Archbold, "Popular Anime That Is Too Messed Up for Hollywood," Looper, June 19, 2017. www.looper.com.

26. Quoted in Robert Epstein, "Spirits, Gods and Pastel Paints: The Weird World of Master Animator Hayao Miyazaki," *The Independent*, January 31, 2010. www.independent.co.uk.

Chapter 3: Something for Everyone

27. Quoted in Sarah Glazer, "Manga for Girls," *New York Times*, September 18, 2005. www.nytimes.com.
28. Jason Thompson, *Manga: The Complete Guide*. New York: Del Rey, 2007.
29. Richard Eisenbeis, "The Five Best Anime of 2014," Kotaku, December 30, 2014. https://kotaku.com.
30. Phelim O'Neill, "*Attack on Titan* Box Set Review—Teens Tangle with People-Eating Giants in This Spellbinding Anime," *The Guardian*, October 16, 2014. www.theguardian.com.
31. Gabriella Eken, "Yuri!!! on Ice: Episode 10," Anime News Network, December 8, 2016. www.animenewsnetwork.com.
32. Tim Jones, "*Gurren Lagann* Review," THEM Anime. https://themanime.org.
33. Quoted in Kitchen Sisters, "Food Manga: Where Culture, Conflict and Cooking All Collide," *Morning Edition,* NPR, August 8, 2016. www.npr.org.

Chapter 4: Essential Anime and Manga

34. Noel Murray, "*Ghost in the Shell*," The Dissolve, September 29, 2014. https://thedissolve.com.
35. Quoted in Steve Rose, "Hollywood Is Haunted by *Ghost in the Shell*," *The Guardian*, October 19, 2009. www.theguardian.com.
36. Maya Phillips, "The 10 Best Anime Shows on Netflix," *Vulture*, October 10, 2017. www.vulture.com.
37. Kristen Yoonsoo Kim, "The Top Five Movies of April 2017," *Brooklyn Magazine*, April 27, 2017. www.bkmag.com.
38. Jason Thompson, "Jason Thompson's House of 1,000 Manga— *Fullmetal Alchemist*," Anime News Network, June 6, 2013. www .animenewsnetwork.com.
39. Caitlin Donovan, "The Women Who Dress like Men: Shoujo Staples of Anime and Manga — Part 2," Mary Sue, August 13, 2014. www .themarysue.com.
40. Quoted in Alex Suskind, "Asteroid Blues: The Lasting Legacy of *Cowboy Bebop*," *The Atlantic*, December 17, 2014. www.the atlantic.com.
41. Morgana Santilli, "The Untold Truth of *Naruto*," Looper, August 28, 2019. www.looper.com.
42. Rose Bridges, "The Secret Revolution of *Ouran High School Host Club*," Anime News Network, September 2, 2015. www.anime newsnetwork.com.

43. Gita Jackson, "Why You Should Watch *JoJo's Bizarre Adventure*," Kotaku, July 5, 2018. https://kotaku.com.
44. Quoted in David McNeill, "Cartoon Friends Strike a Blow for Japanese Women," *The Independent*, August 8, 2012. www.independent.co.uk.
45. Deb Aoki, "Top Shojo Manga Must-Reads," LiveAbout, January 5, 2019. www.liveabout.com.
46. Quoted in Austin Jones and Paste TV Writers, "The 30 Best Anime Series of All Time," *Paste*, June 30, 2020. www.pastemagazine.com.
47. Mike Crandol, "*FLCL* DVD 3 Review," Anime News Network, July 31, 2003. www.animenewsnetwork.com.

Chapter 5: The Future of Anime and Manga

48. Quoted in Dan Meth, "One of the Only Non-Japanese Anime Artists Shares His Experience," BuzzFeed, March 6, 2015. www.buzzfeed.com.
49. Quoted in Brian Ashcraft, "An Insider's Look at Working in the Anime Business," Kotaku Australia, June 26, 2017. www.kotaku.com.au.
50. Quoted in Eric Margolis, "The Dark Side of Japan's Anime Industry," Vox, July 2, 2019. www.vox.com.
51. Quoted in *Hurriyet Daily News*, "Japan's Anime Industry in Crisis," June 17, 2019. www.hurriyetdailynews.com.
52. Quoted in Margolis, "The Dark Side of Japan's Anime Industry."
53. Quoted in Margolis, "The Dark Side of Japan's Anime Industry."
54. Quoted in Isabella Steger, "Too Rich, Too Comfortable: Why Japan Is So Resistant to Change Even as Disaster Looms," Quartz, April 2, 2019. https://qz.com.
55. Quoted in Marc Bain, "How Japan's Global Image Morphed from Military Empire to Eccentric Pop-Culture Superpower," Quartz, May 21, 2020. https://qz.com.
56. Quoted in Cartoon Brew, "Toon Boom Harmony Brings Traditional Anime to Life Digitally," February 7, 2018. www.cartoonbrew.com.
57. Quoted in Vikram Murthi, "Hayao Miyazaki Calls Artificial Intelligence Animation 'An Insult to Life Itself,'" IndieWire, December 13, 2016. www.indiewire.com.
58. Quoted in Margolis, "The Dark Side of Japan's Anime Industry."
59. Quoted in Polygon, "The Best Anime of the Decade," November 6, 2019. www.polygon.com.
60. Quoted in Ajay Shukla, "How Science SARU Animation Studio Is Redefining the Japanese Animation Industry," *Adobe Blog*, May 21, 2020. https://blog.adobe.com.

FOR FURTHER RESEARCH

Books

Steve Alpert, *Sharing a House with the Never-Ending Man: 15 Years at Studio Ghibli*. Berkeley, CA: Stone Bridge, 2020.

Matt Alt, *Pure Invention: How Japan's Pop Culture Conquered the World*. New York: Random House, 2020.

Hector Garcia, *A Geek in Japan: Discovering the Land of Manga, Anime, Zen, and the Tea Ceremony*. North Clarendon, VT: Tuttle, 2019.

Susan Napier, *Miyazakiworld: A Life in Art*. New Haven, CT: Yale University Press, 2018.

Chris Stuckmann, *Anime Impact: The Movies and Shows That Changed the World of Japanese Animation.* Coral Gables, FL: Mango, 2018.

Internet Sources

Eve Gerber interview with Susan J. Napier, "The Best Books on Anime and Manga," Five Books, www.fivebooks.com.

Rich, "Anime's Great Deception – The Difference Between Anime and Cartoons," Tofugu, July 1, 2015. www.tofugu.com.

Alex Suskind, "Asteroid Blues: The Lasting Legacy of Cowboy Bebop," *Atlantic*, December 17, 2014. www.theatlantic.com.

Gunseli Yalcinkaya, "Meet the Creator Behind the First Major Black-Owned Anime Studio," Dazed Digital, August 3, 2020. www.dazeddigital.com.

Websites

Anime News Network (www.animenewsnetwork.com). This is perhaps the most popular online news source for anime, manga, and video games. In addition to news, it provides reviews, press releases, and anime convention reports as well.

CBR (www.cbr.com). CBR covers all comic books, but it also has a great section for anime news. It provides the latest information about anime streaming, the future of individual anime series, and anime-related controversies.

Crunchyroll (www.crunchyroll.com). The news section at Crunchyroll covers the top anime stories, behind-the-scenes articles, reviews, and previews.

Kotaku (https://kotaku.com). Kotaku's section on anime contains articles and news stories. It also covers the best anime cosplays from different conventions.

Tokyo Otaku Mode (https://otakumode.com). This huge site features all kinds of information about Japanese pop culture, including anime, manga, and video games.

INDEX